3.
THE INCLINED PLANE

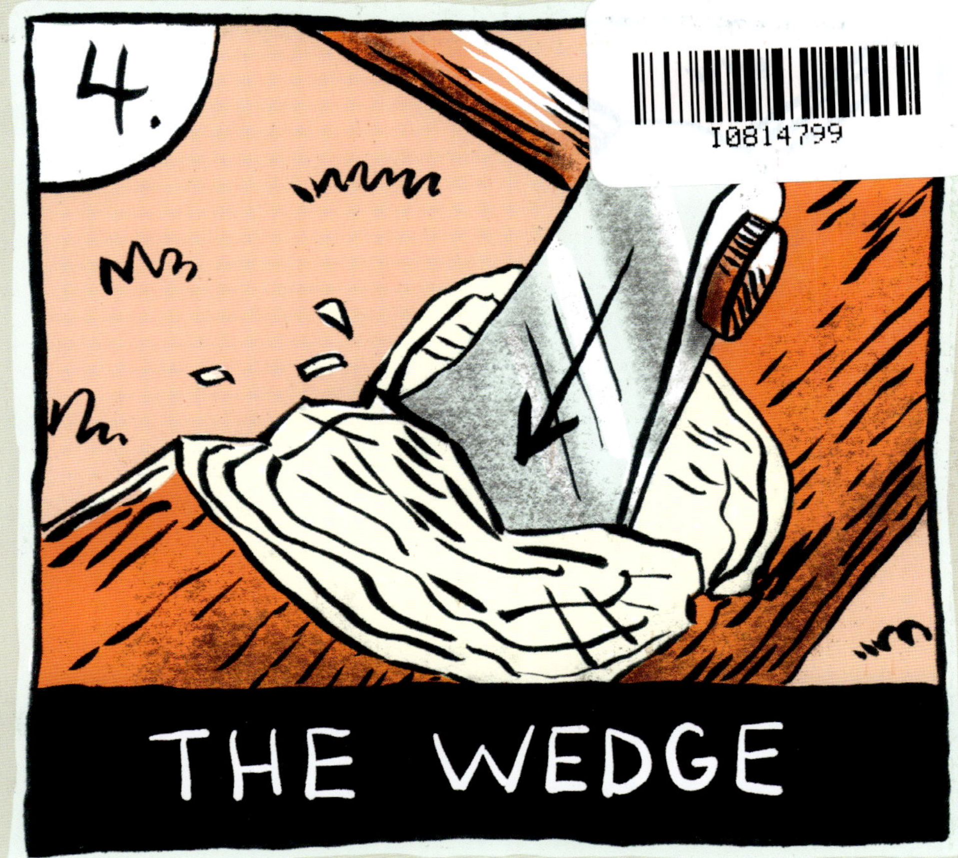
4.
THE WEDGE

5.
THE SCREW

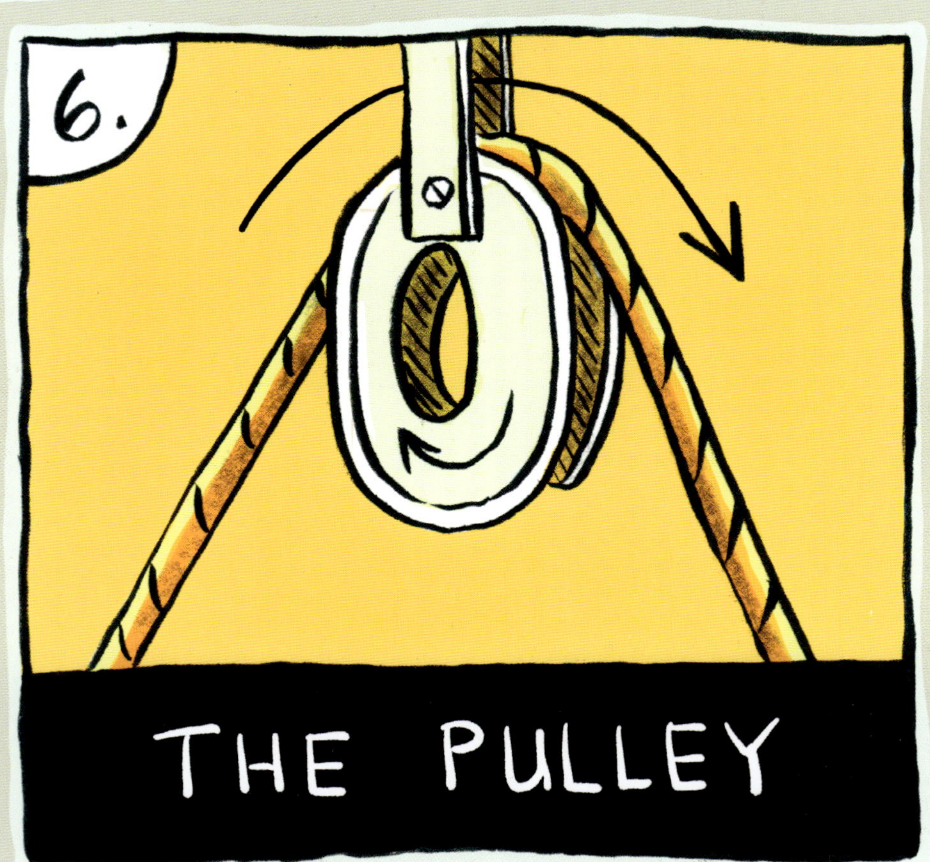
6.
THE PULLEY

Rube Gold·berg *adjective* \'rüb-'gōl(d)-ˌbərg\

: doing something simple in a very complicated way that is not necessary

: accomplishing by complex means what seemingly could be done simply

<a kind of *Rube Goldberg* contraption . . . with five hundred moving parts —L. T. Grant>;

also : characterized by such complex means

For Jude and Beckett—and all your wondrous, hilarious, and ingenious inventiveness to come. Hugs from Ama. —C. T.

To my whole inventive, creative family! —S. M.

YouTube is a trademark of Google LLC.
MythBusters is a trademark of Discovery Communications LLC.
Guinness World Records is a trademark of Guinness World Records Ltd.
Rube Goldberg and Rube Goldberg Machine are trademarks of Rube Goldberg Inc.
Page 33: Rube Goldberg, "Self-Operating Napkin" (detail). Originally published in *Collier's*, September 1931. Public Domain via Wikimedia Commons.

Library of Congress Cataloging-in-Publication Data available.

ISBN 978-1-4521-4422-1

Manufactured in China.

Design by Sara Gillingham Studio.
Typeset in Cronos Pro and Paperboy.
The illustrations in this book were drawn in ink and shaded/colored in Procreate.

10 9 8 7 6 5 4 3 2 1

Chronicle books and gifts are available at special quantity discounts to corporations, professional associations, literacy programs, and other organizations. For details and discount information, please contact our premiums department at corporatesales@chroniclebooks.com or at 1-800-759-0190.

Chronicle Books LLC
680 Second Street
San Francisco, California 94107

Chronicle Books—we see things differently.
Become part of our community at www.chroniclekids.com.

SMASH, CRASH, TOPPLE, ROLL!

THE INVENTIVE RUBE GOLDBERG

A Life in Comics, Contraptions, and Six Simple Machines

By CATHERINE THIMMESH • Illustrated by SHANDA McCLOSKEY

chronicle books · san francisco

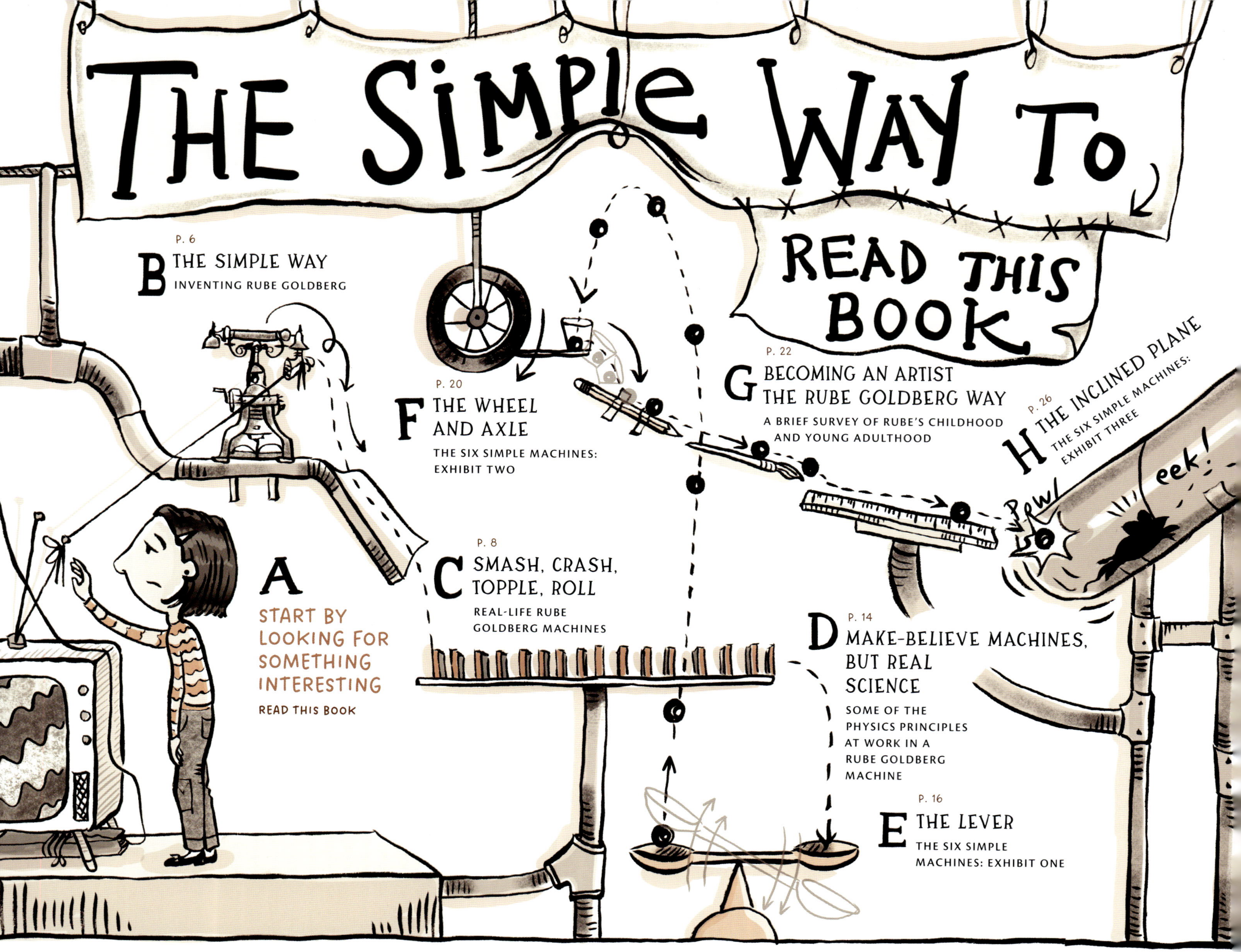

LOOK FOR (A) SOMETHING INTERESTING. WHEN YOU SEE IT, GRAB IT. THE STRING WILL PULL (B) THE RECEIVER OFF THE TELEPHONE AND SLIDE IT DOWN THE RAMP. (C) THE DOMINOS WILL FALL ONE BY ONE UNTIL (D) THE LAST ONE FALLS ONTO ONE SIDE OF (E) THE BALANCED SPOON, SENDING THE MARBLE FLYING UP TO (F) THE CUP ATTACHED TO THE WHEEL, WHICH WILL TIP TO SEND THE MARBLE DOWN (G) THE ART-SUPPLY RAMPS UNTIL IT CRASHES INTO (H) THE MOUSE TUNNEL, SCARING THE MOUSE. THE MOUSE

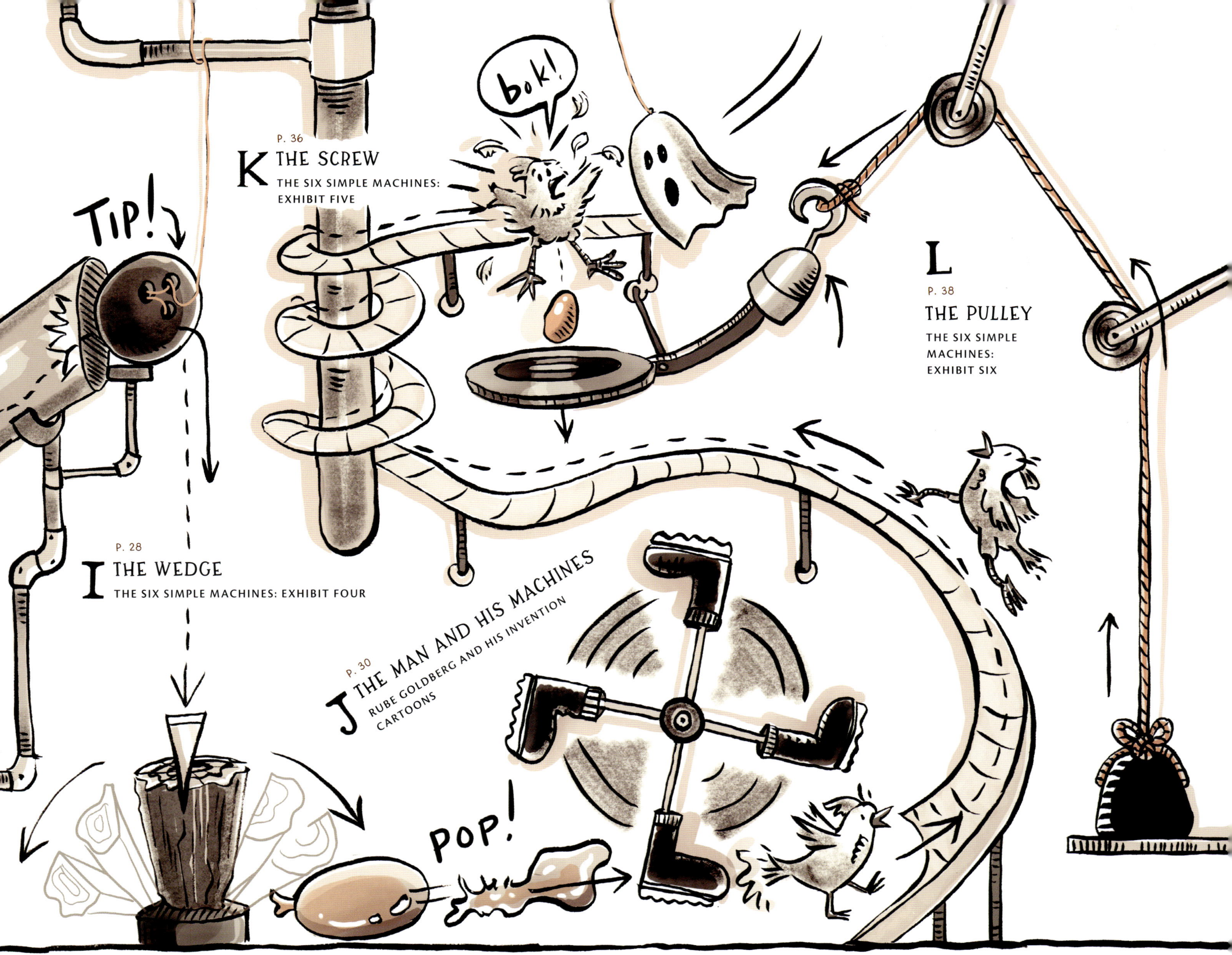

WILL RUN UP TO THE BOWLING BALL AND PUSH IT ONTO (I) THE WEDGE, CHOPPING THE LOG IN HALF. ONE SIDE OF THE LOG WILL FALL ONTO (J) THE BALLOON AND POP IT, KNOCKING THE BOOTS INTO A SPIN THAT WILL KICK THE CHICKEN UP (K) THE SPIRAL RAMP. WHEN THE CHICKEN IS SCARED BY THE GHOST, IT WILL DROP AN EGG ONTO THE TARGET, YANKING (L) THE PULLEYS AND LIFTING THE WEIGHT OFF THE SEESAW...

WHICH WILL MAKE (M) THE DISHES CRASH DOWN ONTO THE BUTTON AND TURN ON (N) THE FAN, SENDING THE PAPERS FLYING INTO THE FACE OF (O) THE MONKEY, CAUSING IT TO DROP ITS BANANAS ONTO (P) THE TRAMPOLINE. THE TRAMPOLINE WILL

BOUNCE THEM ONTO (Q) THE BALANCING SKATEBOARD, WHICH WILL SMASH INTO (R) THE TV AND PULL (S) THE PULLEYS, LIFTING THE BOOK UP TO YOUR EYE LEVEL. THE KNOWLEDGE AND WONDER INSIDE THE BOOK WILL CAUSE BRAIN EXCITEMENT!

THE SIMPLE WAY

Inventing Rube Goldberg

A long time ago—but not *so* long ago, really—the world was different.

There were no computers.

There were no TVs.

There were no radios.

Or cars or buses or planes.

Only a few homes had electricity... and only a few had indoor toilets!

Into this world, on July 4, 1883, Rube Goldberg was born.

He was born on the brink of the greatest technological revolution the world had ever seen. And so Rube had a front-row seat watching the many incredible inventions that popped up—the TV, the car, the plane—a steady stream of exciting (and often quite complicated) machines meant to make life simpler. But all too often, people were left completely befuddled.

The new gadgets were often complicated and sometimes not terribly reliable. This could bring out the worst in people: frustration, anger... some choice words. Rube found this funny. Actually, he found the funny in lots of things. Especially the oddities of the changing world around him: cars and horses transporting people

along the same roads, people with telephones but no one to call (because friends and relatives didn't have them yet), people with electricity while others still used gaslights and candles.

Rube combined his oddball humor and a fascination with the changing world with his artistic talent and became an inventor of crazy contraptions in comic-strip form—inspired by the innovative doohickeys and doodads all around him. He became world-famous.

He became—of all things—an *adjective* in the dictionary.

Rube Goldberg's name became inseparable from his invention cartoons—contraptions designed to accomplish very simple tasks in the most complicated ways possible. And although Rube dreamt up these machines and drew them in detail, he never actually built a working one.

But today, Rube's cartoon drawings have been reinvigorated and reimagined by countless people who were inspired to construct their own real-life, three-dimensional, workable, whimsical contraptions—hundreds of thousands of them!

But why? Why so much interest in machines that seem... well... a bit useless?

Because, really, why do something the simple way... if, instead, there is a catapult option?

SMASH, CRASH, TOPPLE, ROLL

Real-Life Rube Goldberg Machines

The lead singer of a rock band wanted to catapult *himself*. It took some engineering experts a while to convince him that flinging a rock star across a room via catapult was a recipe for disaster.

So the singer (of the band OK Go) had to settle for being tethered with safety lines before being flung into a pile of boxes. His band (and an elite team of engineers) created one of the most epic of all real-life Rube Goldberg contraptions for their music video *This Too Shall Pass* (viewed many *millions* of times on the internet—and still climbing). The working machine had eighty-nine distinct steps that sent pool balls, bowling balls, shopping carts, fans, umbrellas, pianos, and a mishmash of other stuff—lots and lots and lots of other stuff—smashing, crashing, toppling, and rolling smack into the next thing.

Rube Goldberg had no such worries. He was completely free to *create* disasters. He made a pool ball drop through a pocket onto a teeter-totter and bounce the measles germ (a make-believe cartoon animal) skyward to hit a doll. He made a cuckoo clock bird fall onto a seesaw and launch a knife up to pierce a sandbag. He even made an angry Spanish bull catapult a tourist into another country. Since his invention cartoons were solely drawings, he could catapult objects and animals and people with abandon. And he did.

Catapult or no catapult, Rube Goldberg–inspired contraption machines are just plain . . . fun.

To watch.

To design.

To build.

To test.

To rebuild.

To cheer on.

Because of the internet, and YouTube in particular, the popularity of Rube Goldberg Machines has exploded. The folks on the TV show *MythBusters* made one—with, among other things, bowling balls, magnets, toy trains, burning candles, shooting water, and the fizzing reaction from combining Mentos and cola. *Guinness World Records* has an entry for the most steps in a successfully completed Rube Goldberg Machine—a record that changes frequently, given the number of people who seek to break it each year. (One year, the record was 412 steps to light a Christmas tree!)

Suddenly it became easy for individuals to share their fun and hard work, creativity, and ingenuity with their friends and the world. And with each click and each new video—be it six random items crash-boom-banging into each other to eventually pop a balloon or nineteen attempts to make a ten-step machine staple a piece of paper—viewers are inspired and encouraged to create their own contraptions . . . and post their own videos, perhaps inspiring someone else along the way.

In one video, a boy whispers, *"Yes!"* with a big smile and both fists pumping the air.

While the inventions in Rube's cartoon strips were centered around humor and storytelling, the three-dimensional machines being created today (more often than not) are contraptions that tend to focus more on the challenges of the chain reaction itself—the randomness of the disparate parts that smash, crash, topple, and roll smack into the next thing.

In another, a young boy coaxes his machine. *"C'mon, c'mon, marble! Yes!"* he gleefully announces with outstretched arms. *"I didn't make a mistake this time!"*

"Take fifteen . . . ," states a girl, one of several kids trying to turn on a coffee maker with an elaborate chain reaction. *"Yes!"* (Arms raised triumphantly in the air.) *"Look! It's pouring coffee."*

Each effort is different in its elaborateness, but each is magical and thrilling to watch. It's also hard work—because precision is everything. But the possibilities are limitless . . . and therein lies the beauty.

SPOON
CATAPULTS
MARBLE

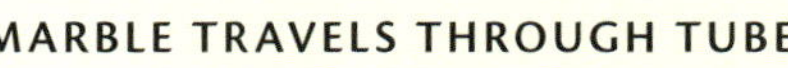

MARBLE TRAVELS THROUGH TUBE

Rube's cartoons also relied quite often on a provoked response from animals or humans—such as a mouse seeing cheese and then jumping to get it, thereby snapping a trap, and then . . . In a cartoon, this seems logical. In real life, predictability is key—and mice can be difficult to train. Real machines need to rely on the physical properties of the objects themselves: A hammer, for example, can smash into something; a bowling ball can drop and roll (but maybe not in a straight line).

And with a bit of imagination, objects can be repurposed. In fact, that's one of the things that makes these contraptions so fun—coming up with clever, new uses for everyday objects: rulers as ramps, toilet-paper rolls as tunnels, soda bottles as funnels, books as dominos, tape rolls as wheels. Who says a straw hat can't work as a bucket? And what exactly *is* a spoon if not the perfect arm for a catapult?

Ultimately, the chain reaction itself is the heart and soul and gold of these machines. That was Rube's real breakthrough. Yes, he had the stories. Yes, the humor. But it was his understanding of the seemingly improbable but delightful nature of the chain reaction—the step-by-step-by-step drama unfolding in quick succession—that truly defined what a Rube Goldberg invention machine was.

Sure, it might take fifteen tries before it works. But then, look . . . a Matchbox car, dominos, and pieces of string are turning on a machine that pours coffee.

STRING PULLS
GLOVE OFF BAT
BAT FALLS
BUCKET PULLS
STRING
TRAIN HITS
BUCKET
BUCKET FALLS
OFF TABLE
IT'S
WORKING!

And *that's* why Rube Goldberg Machines are so popular.

They are thrilling because they do very ordinary (and expected) things in very extraordinary (and unexpected) ways.

They are thrilling because they are *real*.

Not computer-generated.

Not preprogrammed.

Not edited. Not Photoshopped.

Not faked.

Real objects, set up with hands-on precision, relying on creativity and the laws of physics to knock the next thing into the next thing into the next until the machine cycles through the sequence and the task is completed.

It's creative and fun, *and* it's science.

What could be better?

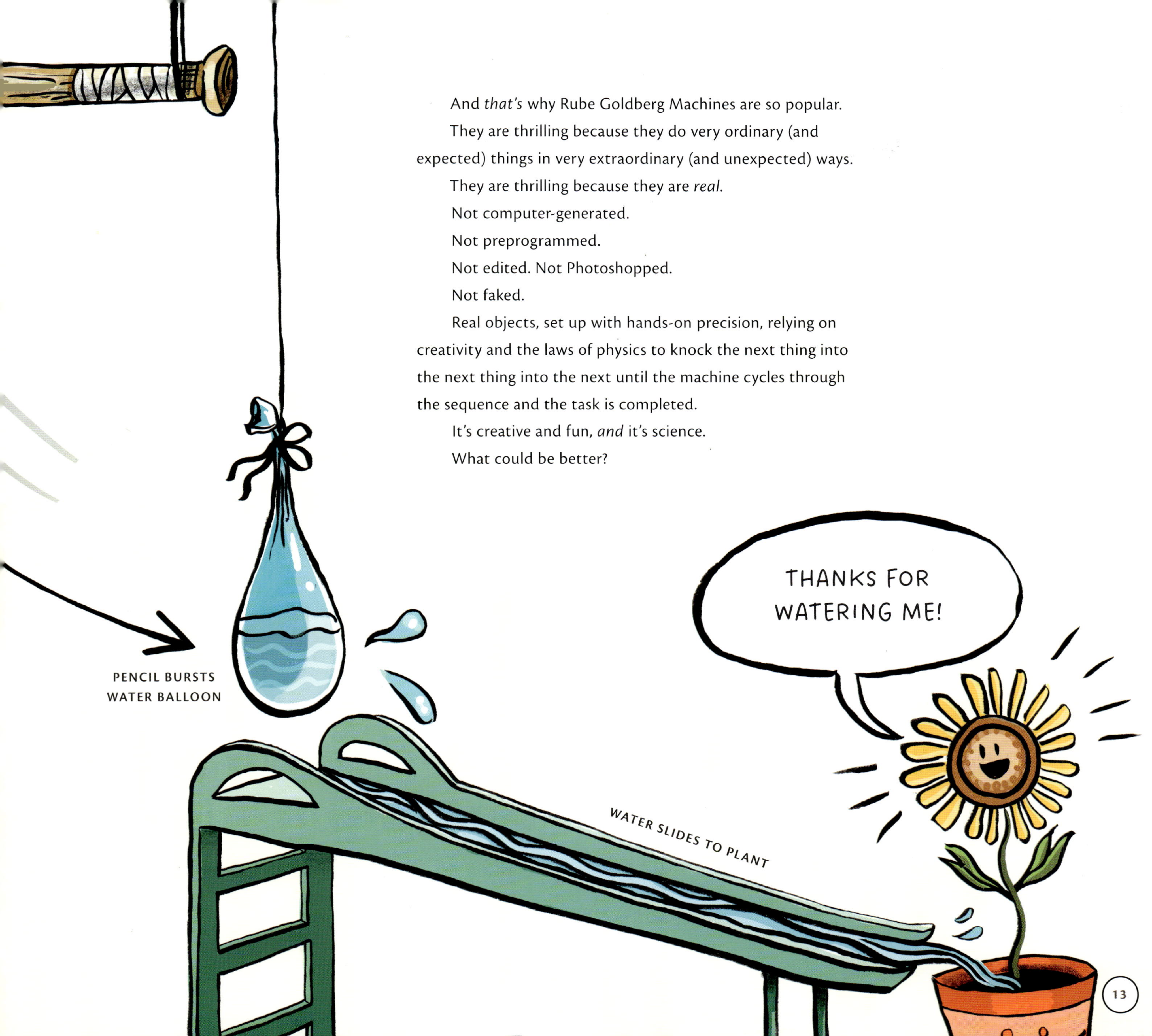

MAKE-BELIEVE MACHINES, BUT REAL SCIENCE

Some of the Physics Principles at Work in a Rube Goldberg Machine

Machines, by definition, do work. And usually, they're meant to *simplify* that work. Rube Goldberg cartoon machines, however, manage to do the complete opposite. A tremendous amount of work is put into making a whimsical machine for accomplishing only the simplest of tasks.

But beneath the whimsy lies the science. Many of the steps within a complicated Goldberg chain reaction are machines themselves, invented by ancient peoples and using the principles of physics in order to make work easier. Most Rube Goldberg contraptions are powered by gravity and some combination of the six simple machines:

a lever,
a wheel and axle,
an inclined plane,
a wedge,
a screw,
and a pulley.

These six simple machines are used to change the direction of force, increase the magnitude (the amount) of force, or transfer a force from one place to another—thus providing a mechanical advantage that makes work seem easier.

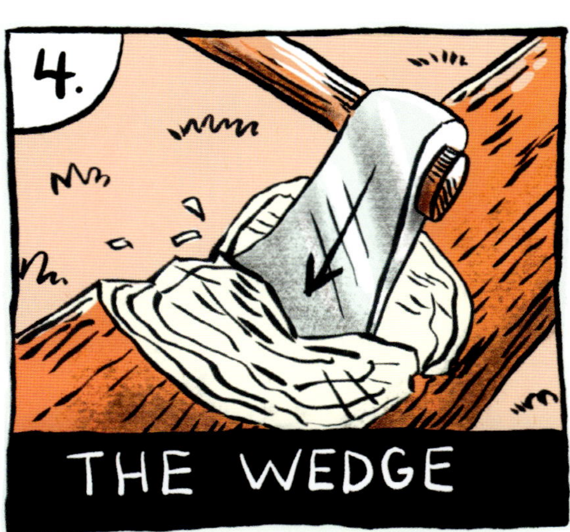

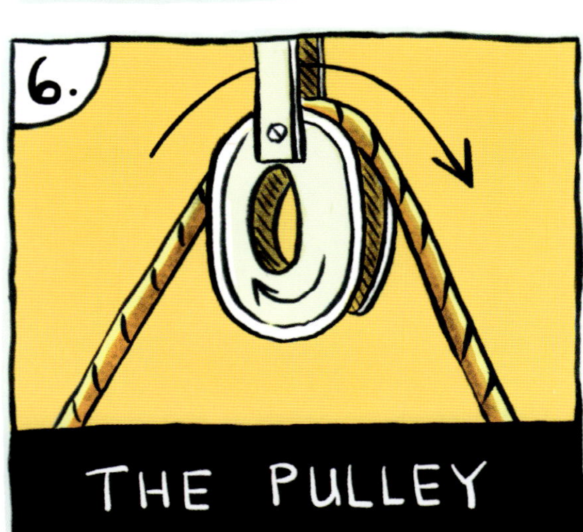

Additional physics concepts at work in Rube Goldberg Machines include types of forces, types of energy, transfer of energy, the law of conservation of energy, the law of conservation of momentum, and Newton's laws of motion.

THE LEVER

The Six Simple Machines: Exhibit One

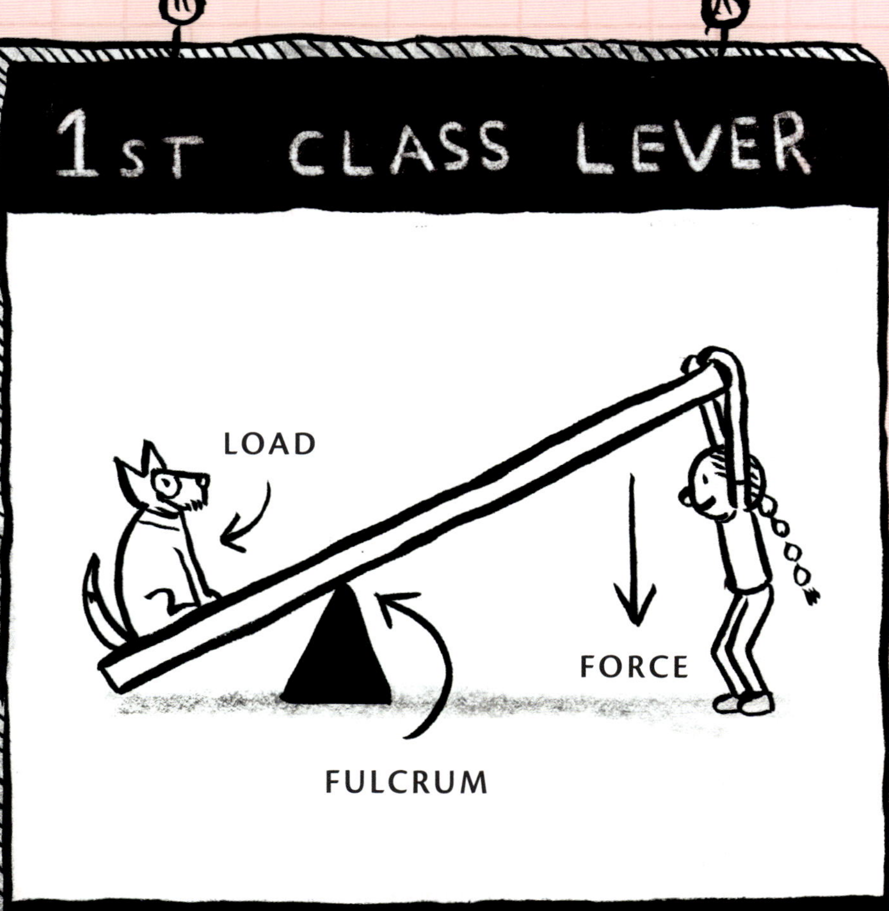

The six simple machines work to pull objects, lift objects, increase force, change direction of force, change direction of motion, or split or cut things apart. The primary benefit of simple machines is that they allow a user to do the same amount of work by using a smaller amount of force spread over a greater distance.

A lever is a rigid bar that rests on a fulcrum (or pivot point). When levers are used to lift a heavy weight, a person gains a mechanical advantage (in which the amount of force they get out of the machine is greater than the amount of force they put in), thus making the work easier. Levers can also be used to move an object a greater distance or increase the speed of an object.

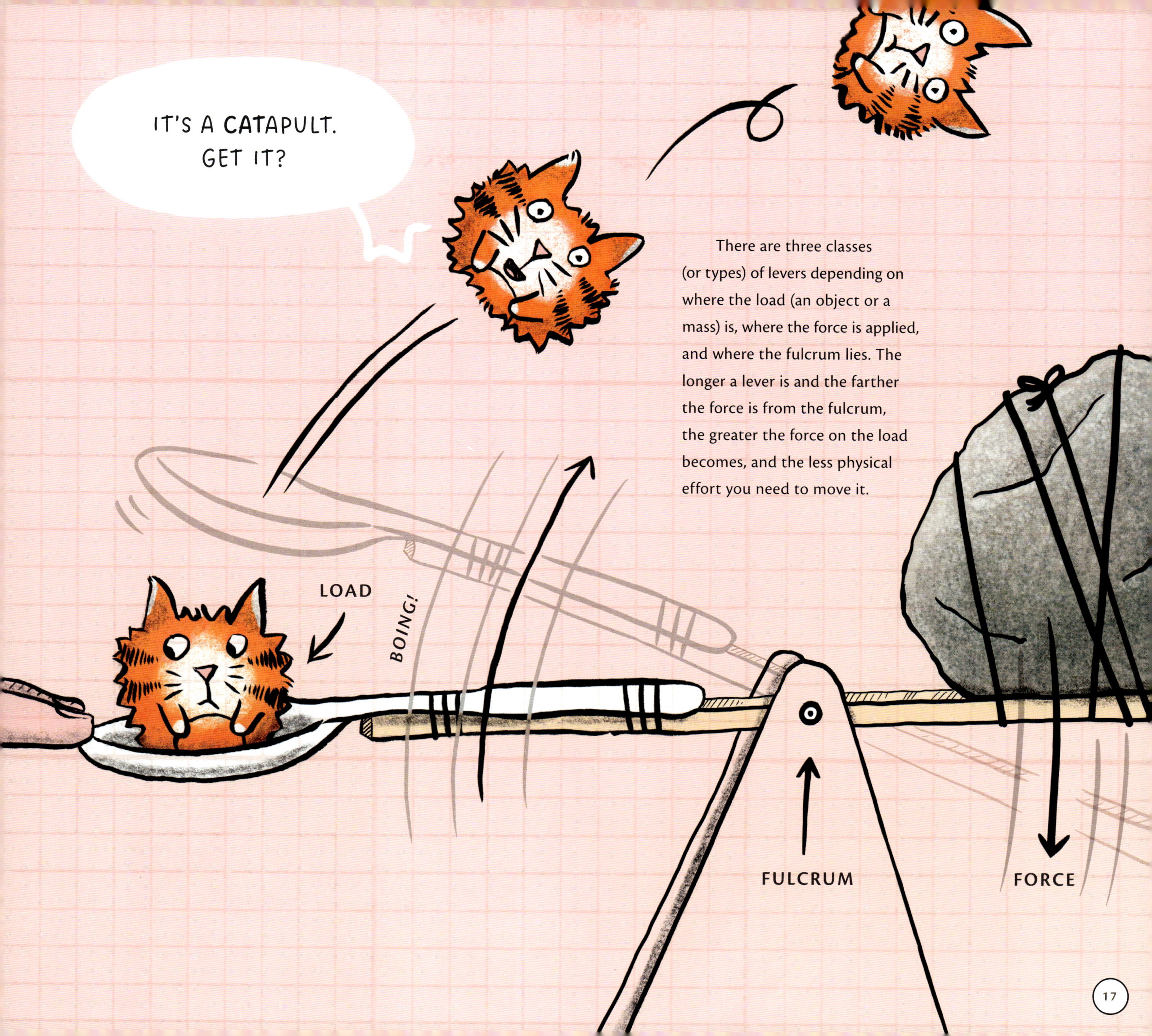

There are three classes (or types) of levers depending on where the load (an object or a mass) is, where the force is applied, and where the fulcrum lies. The longer a lever is and the farther the force is from the fulcrum, the greater the force on the load becomes, and the less physical effort you need to move it.

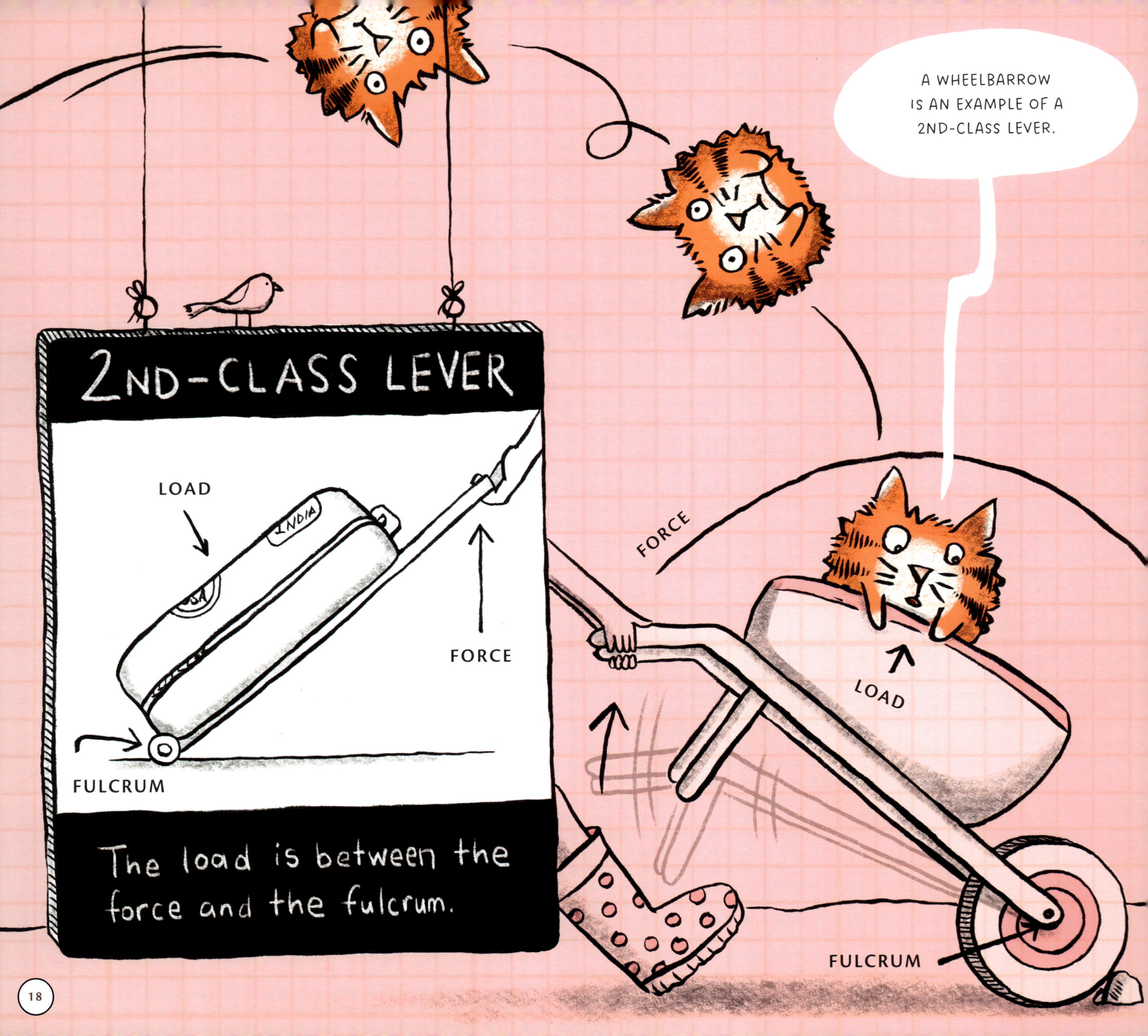
2ND-CLASS LEVER
LOAD
INDIA
FORCE
FULCRUM
The load is between the force and the fulcrum.
A WHEELBARROW IS AN EXAMPLE OF A 2ND-CLASS LEVER.
FORCE
LOAD
FULCRUM

3RD-CLASS LEVER
FORCE
FULCRUM
LOAD
The force is between the load and the fulcrum.
A BROOM IS A 3RD-CLASS LEVER.
FULCRUM
FORCE
LOAD

THE WHEEL AND AXLE

The Six Simple Machines: Exhibit Two

The wheel is considered to be one of the most significant and transformative inventions in the history of the world.

A wheel can spin around a rod, but that rod is not an axle. In a wheel-and-axle machine, an axle is a rod *attached* to the wheel, so if one spins, so does the other. The two objects rotate each other when a force is applied to either one of them.

A greater distance moved at the edge of the wheel is converted to a shorter distance moved at the axle, and vice versa. Conversely, a stronger *force* at the wheel's axle will give a weaker force at the wheel's edge but will move it a greater distance, and vice versa. Instead of simply moving—dragging—a load, a wheel lets you move the point of contact with the ground, which cuts down on the amount of friction between the surface and the load you are moving.

A wheel and axle can also be used like a lever. They rotate around a fixed point that acts as a rotating lever. The center where the axle turns is the fulcrum of the rotating lever, and the wheel is the outer part of the lever. A doorknob, for example, is a wheel and axle that is essentially a round lever.

FORCE APPLIED TO THE WHEEL (WHEN THE BALL FALLS IN THE CUP) CAUSES THE AXLE TO TURN WITH GREATER FORCE THAN THE WHEEL.
A WHEEL AND AXLE OVERCOME THE FORCES OF GRAVITY AND FRICTION TO MAKE MOVING A HEAVY LOAD EASIER.
LOAD
EFFORT
WHEEL
AXLE

BECOMING AN ARTIST THE RUBE GOLDBERG WAY

A Brief Survey of Rube's Childhood and Young Adulthood

Rube loved to draw. As far back as he could remember, Reuben Garrett Lucius Goldberg (aka Rube) loved putting pen to paper—and he did. He also put pen to walls, to his parents' books, to anything within reach. Using the translucent paper set aside by his mother for her dressmaking, he traced picture after picture after picture from his favorite books.

His parents, however, weren't terribly enthusiastic about his love of art. They didn't particularly encourage his passion—and in fact, as he grew older, they actively discouraged him from pursuing art professionally. As Rube put it, *"No one in my family showed any interest in the creative arts. Somehow it was in my bones..."*

But it didn't matter. Rube *had* to draw. He would make it happen.

When Rube was around eleven years old, he and a friend hired a sign painter to teach them drawing and other art techniques. Every Friday night for over two years, the kids had a private lesson with the painter. (Rube would later say he spent his weeks eagerly waiting for Friday nights to come along.) Each of the boys paid fifty cents per lesson. Rube paid for his lessons with money from his own pocket.

Of that experience, Rube remarked, *"I never forgot what he [Charles Beall, the sign painter] taught me. [He] taught me the secrets of success in art—and everything else. He taught me to work."*

And work, Rube did. He drew in charcoal and in pencil and with pen dipped in ink. He sloshed brushes into watercolors and oil paints. His dedication catapulted him to his first solo art exhibition—at age twelve: a studiously drawn portrait of a violinist that was hung for display in his grammar school. By the time he reached high school, his drawings were regular features in the school newspaper. In college, he churned out a steady stream of artwork for the campus humor magazine.

These drawings for the humor magazine were created during whatever free hours he had. Much of his time in college was spent studying science. He graduated from the University of California, Berkeley, with a degree in mining engineering—a pathway chosen not by him, but *for* him, by his father.

According to Rube, his dad told him that *"all cartoonists were good-for-nothing Bohemians and couldn't make a living drawing pictures."* And it was that philosophy that sent him tumbling down the educational pathway chosen for him by his father.

But unbeknownst to Rube at the time, it was a pathway rich with hidden treasure. Looking back, he said, *"My knowledge of science and mechanics is largely responsible for my progress as a cartoonist[!]"*

Rube didn't realize it then, but as he later told the story, one of his analytical engineering classes left an indelible mark. All it took was one overly serious professor with a preposterous idea—to determine the weight of the planet Earth—and an equally preposterous contraption that the professor had built called the Barodik.

"You had to find the weight of the Earth with this contraption," Rube explained. *"There was a whole room full of retorts and Bunsen burners and beakers and motors. . . . There was nothing more ridiculous to me than finding the weight of the Earth."*

The Barodik was apparently so ludicrous, so absurd in its complexity, such an impossible tool to actually calculate the weight of the Earth, that Rube found it a hilarious exercise, if not an outright farce. He claims the students spent six months fiddling with this contraption, and no answer was more wrong—or more accurate—than another, since realistically you simply could not find the weight of the Earth with the Barodik (never mind that the Earth would actually be measured in terms of mass, not weight).

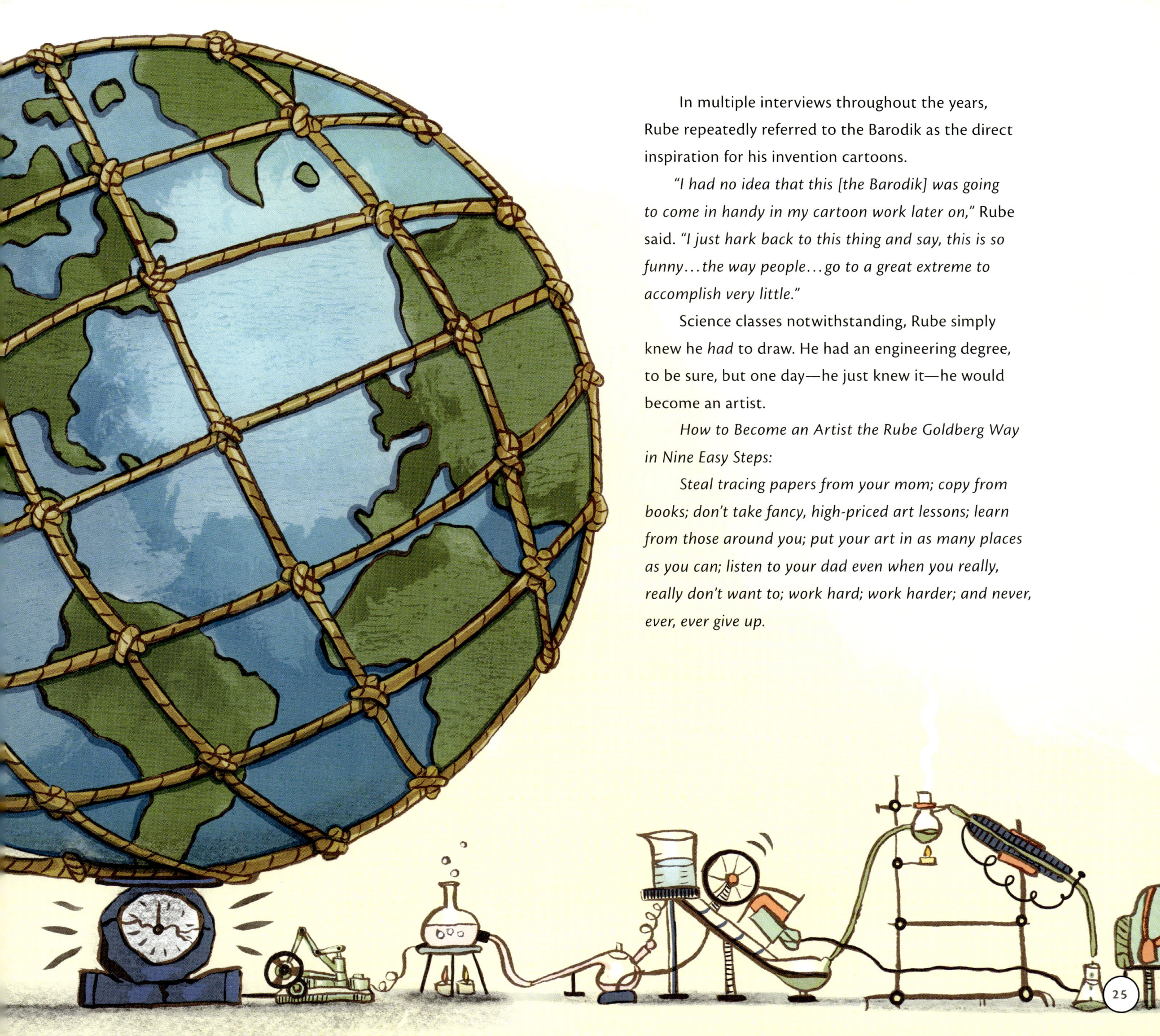

In multiple interviews throughout the years, Rube repeatedly referred to the Barodik as the direct inspiration for his invention cartoons.

"I had no idea that this [the Barodik] was going to come in handy in my cartoon work later on," Rube said. *"I just hark back to this thing and say, this is so funny . . . the way people . . . go to a great extreme to accomplish very little."*

Science classes notwithstanding, Rube simply knew he *had* to draw. He had an engineering degree, to be sure, but one day—he just knew it—he would become an artist.

How to Become an Artist the Rube Goldberg Way in Nine Easy Steps:

Steal tracing papers from your mom; copy from books; don't take fancy, high-priced art lessons; learn from those around you; put your art in as many places as you can; listen to your dad even when you really, really don't want to; work hard; work harder; and never, ever, ever give up.

THE INCLINED PLANE

The Six Simple Machines: Exhibit Three

An inclined plane is a simple machine that consists of a flat surface raised at an angle. The best example is a ramp. Use of an inclined plane is a way to lift or lower a load—making an otherwise heavy or cumbersome load more easily managed by the person moving it. It changes the way the work is done by increasing or decreasing the amount of force needed to move the load, depending on the steepness of the slope. The steeper the ramp, the more force needed to move the load up, and the less force needed to move it down.

Inclined planes offer a trade-off between force applied and distance/time. If the ramp is steep, it takes more force to move the load up, but the distance the load travels (and the time it takes to do so) is short. When the ramp has a gentle slope, it takes less force to move the load up, but the distance it travels (and the time it takes to do so) is greater.

An object going down an inclined plane will accelerate due to the force of gravity as long as the force in the direction of motion is greater than the force of friction holding it in place. The steeper the slope, the faster the object slides down.

THE WEDGE

The Six Simple Machines: Exhibit Four

A wedge is a simple machine made up of two planes, one of which needs to be inclined (or tilted), that meet together and form a sharp edge. But whereas an inclined plane is stationary, the wedge accomplishes work because it is movable.

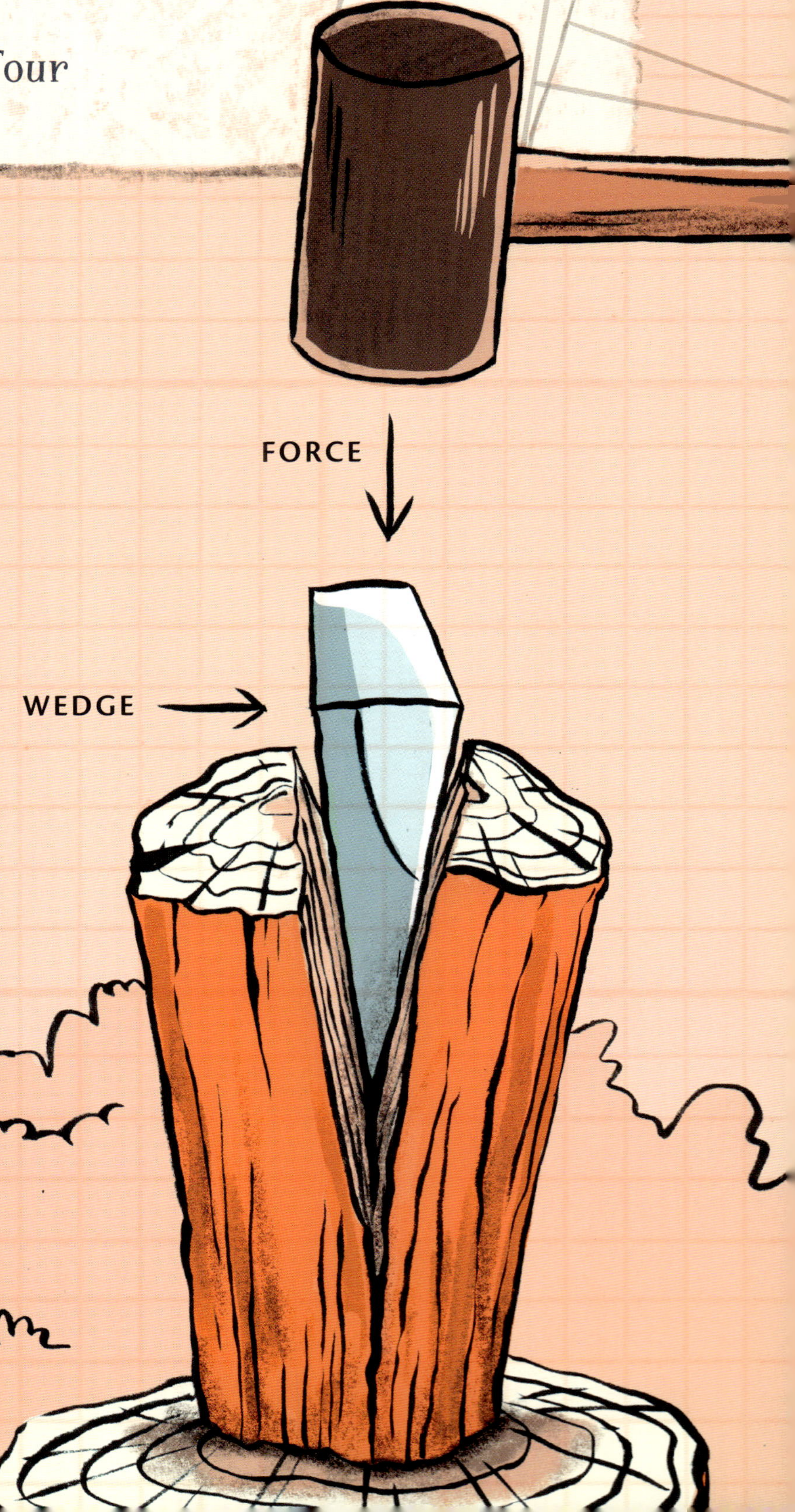

Because a wedge is movable, it can be driven under a load to lift it (like a shovel tip), or it can be driven into a load to separate or split it (like a chisel), or it can be driven under a load to lift and hold an object in place (like a doorstop). The wedge accomplishes these things by changing the direction of the force: For example, a downward, vertical force on a wedge produces a horizontal output force within the object.

THE MAN AND HIS MACHINES

Rube Goldberg and His Invention Cartoons

PEOPLE COMING INTO MY STUDIO EXPECT ME TO BE HANGING FROM THE CHANDELIER.

Rube wrote in 1961, *"It is always a disappointment to them and me, too, that I am a perfectly normal human being."*

Still, he was a human being who proposed that the "only successful way of hailing a street car" involved a chicken, a rubber bulb, a saw, some string, a pulley, and—among other things—a flying fish.

But Rube *was* a perfectly normal human being for a man in the 1920s: He loved cars (he was one of the first to own a car in New York City, when there were only a dozen on the road), wore bow ties and other fancy attire, smoked cigars, loved being the center of attention, and wore shoes when he went swimming. OK, that last one's not particularly normal . . . but still, he wasn't particularly odd.

Eight long years before Rube Goldberg published his first contraption cartoon—a "mosquito exterminator," which required the mosquito to walk a plank, eat steak, look through a telescope, and jump off a springboard (ultimately leading to its death)—he landed his first newspaper job.

It was 1904. Rube sprang from college with his engineering degree, fell right into his first job as a city engineer (where he spent six short miserable months), and took a leap of faith by quitting that job and knock-knock-knocking on newspaper doors until finally one swung open at the *San Francisco Chronicle*, allowing him to slide into a position with the sports pages. A newspaper job. It wasn't his dream job, but still, he was getting paid to draw cartoons!

But where he truly longed to be was New York City—the capital of the publishing world. It was there that he wanted to launch a career as a humor cartoonist.

So one day—after an eight-month stint at the *Chronicle* and two years at the *San Francisco Bulletin* (primarily as a sports cartoonist)—he quit and went off cross-country in pursuit of his dream.

New York greeted him harshly: Rejection followed rejection, after rejection and more rejection. But Rube's persistence paid off, and he was eventually hired at the *New York Evening Mail*—first as a sports cartoonist, and a short time later as a general humorist.

"The first thing that I did that attracted real attention," said Rube, *"was* Foolish Questions *and that was an accident."*

By "accident," he meant that he drew a one-panel, meant-to-be-one-time cartoon that was published in the *Evening Mail*. And then, much to his surprise, the very next day he was bombarded with phone calls and overwhelmed with mail that not only praised the cartoon but also begged for additional segments—even offering ideas for the next "foolish question" he just had to illustrate.

"Young man, did you fall?" inquires a man standing on the street, looking down at a man lying on the ground tangled up in a bicycle. The reply: *"No—I'm taking a little nap."*

It's easy to see the universal appeal—who hasn't suffered through someone asking a question for which the answer is so blatantly obvious? Rube would go on to illustrate over 450 *Foolish Questions* panels—and they rocketed Rube Goldberg straight to national fame.

He had his second massive hit just two years later with the comic strip *I'm the Guy.* (The theme was lifted from a line he heard at a vaudeville performance: "I'm the guy who put the salt in the ocean.")

Then, in 1912, Rube published the first of what would become twenty years' worth of invention cartoons—and hit upon the crucial winning combination right from the get-go. Instinctively, he knew that the very process of reaching the end—the chain-reaction steps themselves—was much more compelling than the actual end result of a completed task.

When asked by random people in everyday encounters how he thought up each individual invention, Rube replied, *"I don't know. I do know that I want to express a simple everyday thing in the most complicated and humorous way I know. So I do it."*

He may not have been able to pinpoint his idea-generating process, but clearly Rube drew inspiration from the steady stream of inventions that populated his day-to-day world. He routinely saved newspaper clippings announcing the patents awarded for the latest inventions—with hard-to-resist headlines that declared "Inventor Who Had a Stiff Back Gets Patent on Pants Remover" and "Umbrella with a View" and "A Non-Spill Pocket."

Rube also collected actual patent applications from other people's inventions (from the US Patent and Trademark Office, and also from those published in newspapers). His method of labeling the steps in his machines alphabetically (A goes to B, which goes to C, etc.) came straight out of the patent office's method for labeling schematic drawings.

A person could be forgiven for confusing some of the crazier patent drawings for a Rube Goldberg cartoon—and vice versa—since stylistically, they were quite similar.

It is no surprise, then, that at *least* one Goldberg invention machine (though there are most certainly others) can be directly connected to its most likely source: US patent #1,046,533, awarded to one Arnold Zukor on December 12, 1912, for a burglar alarm, found among Rube's personal papers. The burglar alarm "can be readily adapted to a door or window" and will awaken the sound sleeper—alerting them to an intrusion—"in the form of a water spray" that comes from a nozzle fixed above the bed.

I WANT TO EXPRESS A SIMPLE EVERYDAY THING IN THE MOST COMPLICATED AND HUMOROUS WAY I KNOW. SO I DO IT.

From there, Arnold Zukor's patented invention employs window sashes, rails, nuts and bolts, gears, pulleys, faucets, rods, actuating levers, springs, and, of course, a nozzle spray. It takes up the entire room.

Nearly twenty years later, we find a Rube Goldberg invention cartoon for a "simple alarm clock." The room layout is almost identical to the one depicted on the patent application for the burglar alarm, with the bed parallel to the window and the alarm gadget overtaking the room. Rube's invention takes sixteen steps to wake the sleeper, using a balloon, a brick, a perfumed sponge, a string, a cannonball, and a vacuum bottle to drop ice water on the snuggled-up snoozer.

And just as Rube sought inspiration from patent records (and the newspapers), it's entirely plausible that some of *today's* inventions drew upon Rube's cartoons. He did design an automatic garage-door opener at least twenty years before the real thing materialized, and his selfie cartoon ("Simple Device for Taking Your Own Picture") was created in 1930! (Of course, Rube's versions weren't exactly marketable.)

Rube also understood the humor inherent in stringing incongruous objects together—and the surprises he could elicit when juxtaposing a mishmash of stuff together. And no matter how convoluted or crazy the contraption, Rube was always meticulous in his step-by-step instructions; each step followed a narrative logic that made perfect sense in context (even if liberties were taken with the laws of nature and physics).

His invention cartoons resonated with readers because Rube had a knack for understanding people and the simple, everyday problems they faced—like how to actually get yourself out of bed in the morning or how to take a picture of yourself when no one's around to do it for you.

But ironically, most people didn't "get" him: the man, separate from his machines. He wasn't a loony hanging from the chandeliers. Nor, it turns out, was he a mechanical whiz—as he once confessed in a TV interview.

"And the funny part of it is that I'm not much of a mechanic," Rube said. *"I don't really have any interest in trying to figure things out the way I'm reputed to do."*

So when something broke down in Rube's home, there was no jury-rigging an eighteen-step inventive solution to the problem... instead, he just called in a neighbor to fix it. Just like plenty of perfectly normal people would.

The inventions he created in his art, though, were anything but normal, and one day the two-dimensional confines of the comic-strip box would prove insufficient to contain all the creativity and innovation these machines had to offer. (Hint: That day is here.)

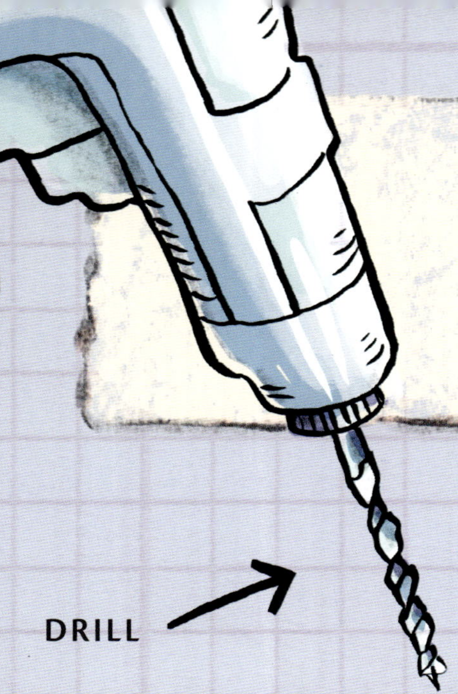

THE SCREW

The Six Simple Machines: Exhibit Five

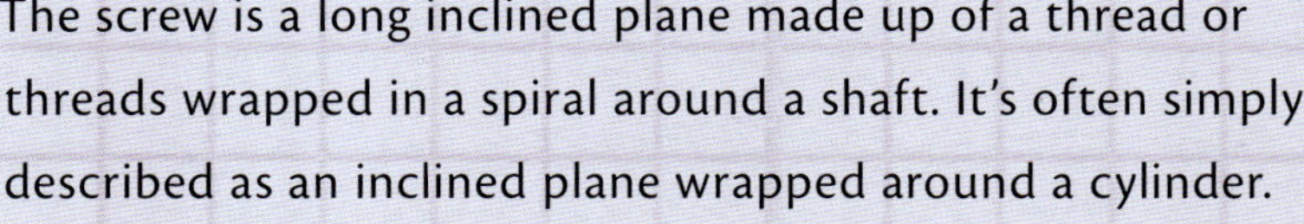

The screw is a long inclined plane made up of a thread or threads wrapped in a spiral around a shaft. It's often simply described as an inclined plane wrapped around a cylinder.

A screw converts a force that goes around and around (a rotational force) into a force that goes up and down or side to side (a linear force).

Screws can also thread into objects so the two objects are interlocked and can't come apart. The strength of the hold depends in large part on the width of the threads and the distance between them (as well as on things like the material of the screw, the diameter of the screw, the shape of the threads, etc.). The closer and wider the threads, the stronger the hold.

Screws used to join two objects together are static systems, and screws used to move objects (as they do in Rube Goldberg Machines) are dynamic systems.

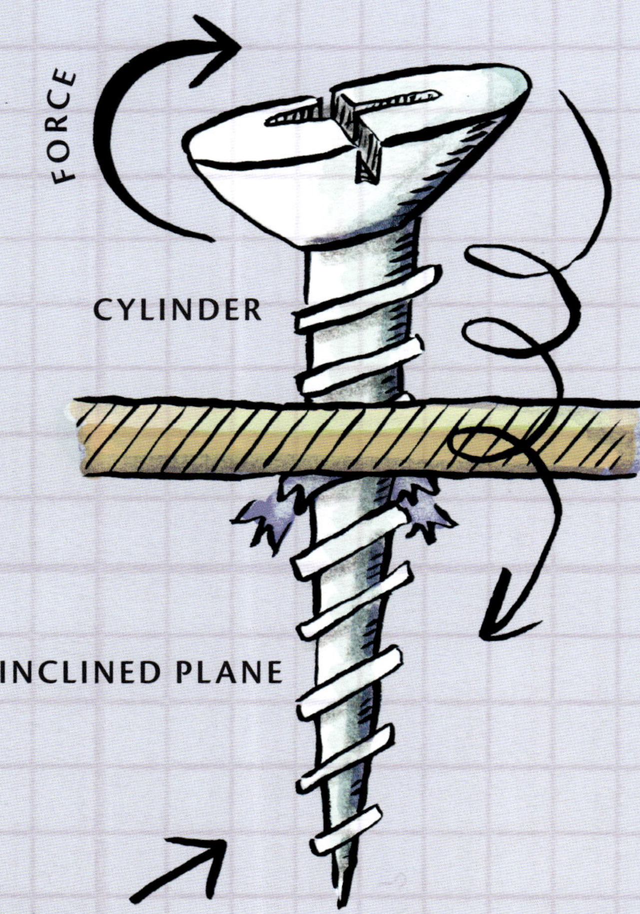

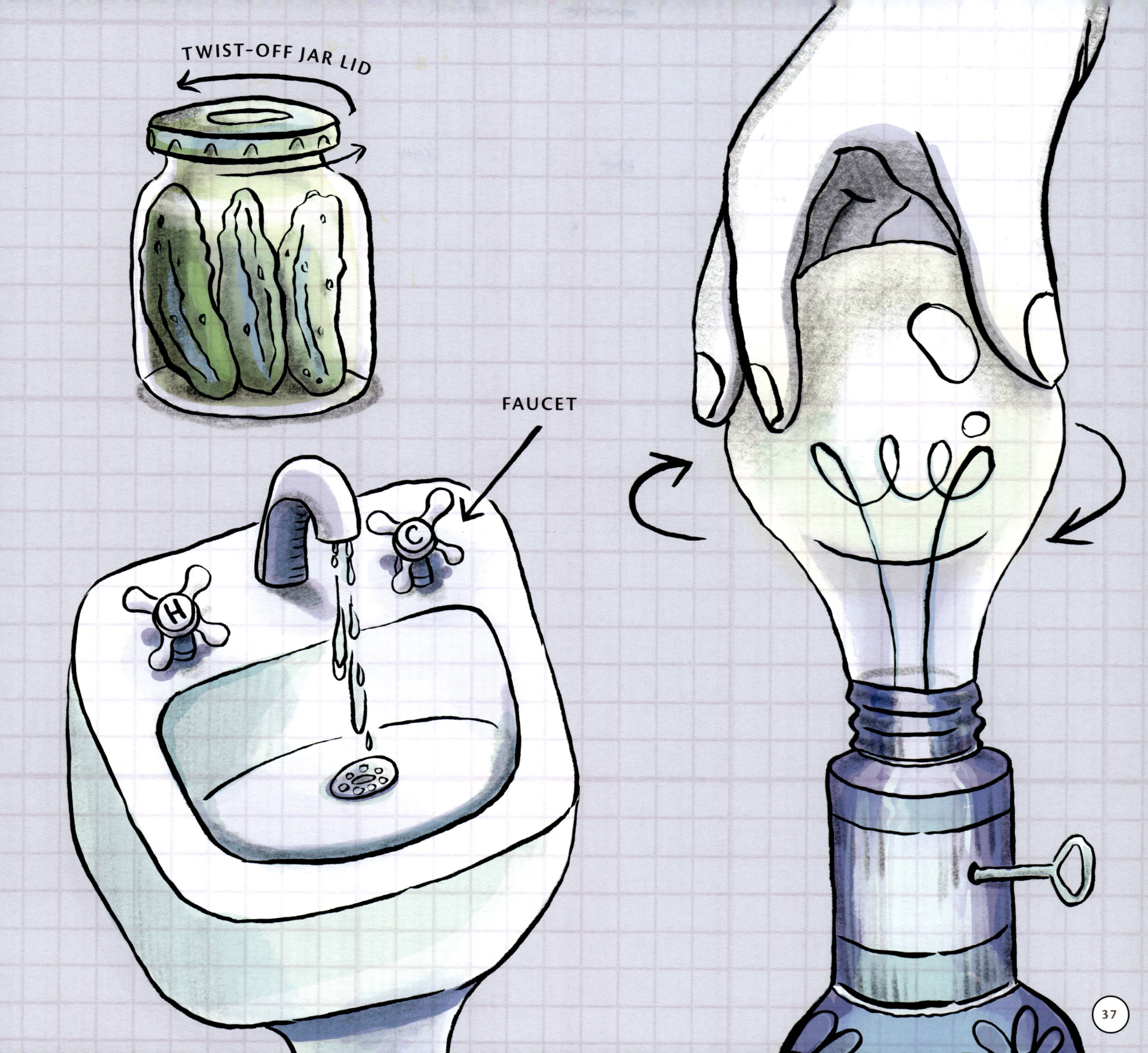
TWIST-OFF JAR LID
FAUCET
H
C

THE PULLEY

The Six Simple Machines: Exhibit Six

A basic pulley consists of a wheel that is fixed upon an axle (a rigid bar). The wheel guides a cable or rope, producing movement. Pulleys allow you to move loads up, down, or sideways.

In a simple pulley, nothing is gained in force, speed, or distance—only the direction of force and possibly motion are changed. A pulley can often make the work of lifting a heavy load seem easier because the direction of motion changes to work with, rather than against, gravity.

By using multiple pulleys together—in a system—the mechanical advantage is increased, allowing much less force to lift a greater load. With a multiple-pulley system, the trade-off is that while you are decreasing the force needed to lift the load, you are also increasing the distance over which the force must be applied.

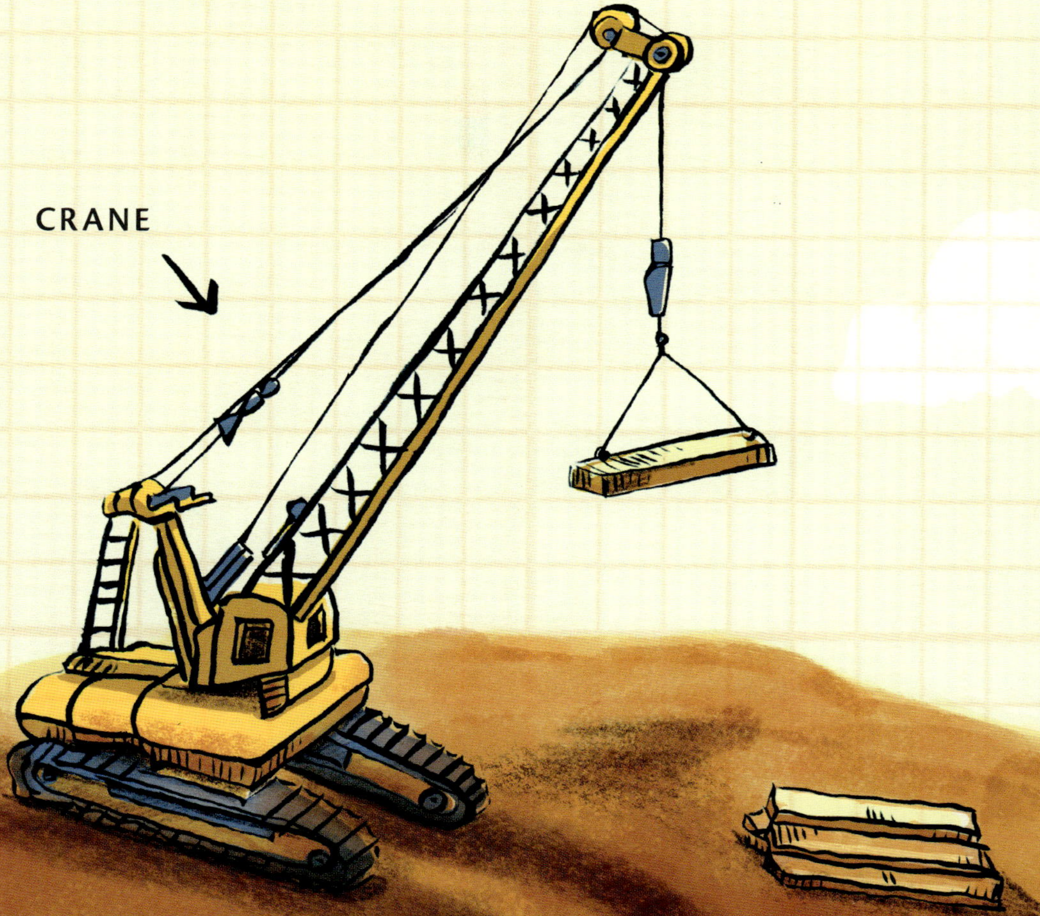

Set It Up; Knock It Down

How to Build a Rube Goldberg Machine

Catapult or no catapult, Rube Goldberg Machines are just plain fun. Folks have seen the videos—toy trucks knocking down books that fall onto spatulas that fling stuff; they know. But the excitement and the wow factor grow exponentially when someone is an active participant...when they are the one doing the designing and the building and the testing and the rebuilding and the cheering-on.

But where to begin? *How* to begin?

1. START AT THE FINISH

There are two distinct pathways to consider when creating a Rube Goldberg contraption machine—and both begin at the same place: the end.

First, this question must be answered: What is the task to accomplish? At the end of the chain reaction, what should happen? Will a plant be watered? A zipper zipped? A ball kerplunked into a bucket?

2. CHOOSE AN APPROACH

There's the more methodical pathway of plotting and planning each of the steps and the interactions and the triggers; but even with this method, there is a certain amount of trial and error that factors in. The less structured approach is to simply begin with trial and error—setting things up and knocking them down. Ultimately, with both methods, the designing and the building will happen in tandem, just to varying degrees.

The fact is, you can measure and map out and build and position with precision, but until the machine elements are actually seen physically interacting with one another, it's nearly impossible to know if the contraption will work properly or not. Tweaking the chain-reaction steps is just part of the process. Set it up. Knock it down. Make adjustments. Try again.

The trial-and-error method generally works just fine if the machine is only a few steps. But the more complicated the machine—the more steps and triggers in the chain reaction—the more helpful the initial planning will be.

3. BRAINSTORM

What items will you incorporate? What will be the steps in the chain reaction?

4. SKETCH

Creating a rough drawing of which object will roll into what, triggering which object to fall, etc., is a helpful way to refine your ideas. Think about the properties of the objects—how they act and react. What angles and levels will the objects need to be placed at to work?

Think about how to use the simple machines and where they'll be placed, and how they'll be used to transfer momentum and energy. Think about using gravity to move the objects: Build the contraption on different levels—different heights—to utilize the drop that gravity gives.

5. BUILD

Start putting your machine together, modifying along the way. Tip: It's helpful to build just a couple of steps at a time, testing the triggers as you go. Also very helpful is marking the exact locations of your objects and setups (with tape or pencil marks)—so if something is moved, it can be put back precisely where it was.

6. TEST

Try the whole thing out! Then identify problems and possible solutions. Testing, rebuilding, testing, rebuilding again (and again)—these are part of the process of building Rube Goldberg Machines. And with a Rube Goldberg Machine, failure—especially a spectacular *crash-boom-bang*—amps up the chaos... and the fun.

7. LEARN

Set it up. Knock it down. Learn from it. Failure is the key to eventual success.

Rube even worked failure into some of his cartoons. In one, "Simple Way to Open a Tight Window," he concluded by stating that after several failed attempts to make the contraption work, the user should pick up the nearby hammer and smash out the glass—thereby opening the window.

Even Rube had a backup plan.

8. EMBRACE MURPHY'S LAW

If anything can go wrong, it will. Because oh, yeah, things will go wrong. Even after designing and building and redesigning and rebuilding until everything works...put your machine in front of a class or a competition or in front of family or friends, and something will decide to go wrong again. One of the triggers won't go off. Something will fall off its track. Count on it. Be prepared to troubleshoot. And then don't worry about it.

SOME TIPS

While every Rube Goldberg Machine is its own cleverly constructed contraption, there are several laws of physics incorporated into all of them. For example, as previously noted, most machines (of the Goldberg-esque type) maximize the use of gravity throughout. They rely on kinetic motion, transfer of energy, and transfer of momentum to propel each step in the sequence. Gravity—a force at work on all objects at all times—is an efficient and easy go-to source of energy.

If something is dropped, or shoved down a ramp, gravity's pull will always try to bring it to the ground. If something (or someone) is catapulted across the room, count on gravity to keep it (or them) from flying willy-nilly off into space.

"The two most common concepts that are used universally in the competition [of Rube Goldberg Machines] are falling weights and rolling objects," says Adam Bahrainwala of Purdue University's winning 2014 team. *"Falling weight is a good way to get energy in a small space."*

The six simple machines are perfect for producing or transferring energy. *"Many of the simple machines are the best concepts to use,"* says Adam. *"They are simple enough that you can use them in new and interesting ways."*

It helps to put the smaller and less reliable pieces first in the chain reaction and the most reliable steps (usually involving larger objects) at the end. That way if there's a mishap, it will often happen at the start of the sequence, and it will take less time to reset the machine.

Choosing odd, whimsical objects to complete the machine is half the fun—like using an ice cream scoop as a catapult or tilting a picture frame into an inclined plane. Repurposing everyday objects is where individual creativity, cleverness, and humor really get a chance to shine through. What else could a box be? Or a book? A shoe? A hamster wheel?

This is what Rube always did in his invention cartoons—he constructed them out of everyday items (or people or animals) used in wholly original ways.

"If you take a common item that people don't give a second thought to," says Adam, *"and repurpose it into something really unique, you can get some interesting reactions."*

But perhaps the best tip? Flexibility.

Flexibility is key to success. If something isn't working as envisioned, being adaptable and finding work-arounds to the problems that spring up will ultimately help you create not only an innovative machine but a successfully *working* machine as well. Learn to improvise.

If, like Rube Goldberg, you tell a story with your machine, fantastic! If you can bring the funny—or the crazy or the chaotic—fabulous! If the focus is simply the objects, the steps, and the chain reaction, awesome!

Anything goes. And that's precisely why the designing and building and testing and rebuilding and cheering-on are worth the effort.

And remember, chances are high—really, really high—that it won't work the first time. But that's OK; that's what's supposed to happen. It's not as much fun if you don't get to rethink, revise, and rebuild.

It might not even work on the fifth try. But soon enough, you will find yourself muttering and yelling and urging on the machine as it smashes, crashes, topples, and rolls on to victory: *"Keep going, keep going . . . Come on, come on, come on . . . You can do it!"*—occasionally peppered with loud bursts of *"Oh, no! NO!"*

That's all part of the Rube Goldberg Machine–making process. That last step—the cheering-on—that's the *really* fun part. Because it is all *so* real. And sooner or later, guaranteed, you will find yourself shouting, *"YESSSSSSSSS!"*—probably with arms raised victoriously and a fist pump to top it off.

THIS LOOKS PERFECT!
WHAT COULD GO WRONG?
RUBE
RULES

TOYS

AFTERWORD

SIXTY YEARS AND FIFTY THOUSAND COMIC STRIPS

Some Highlights of Rube Goldberg's Career beyond the Invention Cartoons

Over the years (from 1904 to 1964), Rube Goldberg penned at least seventy different comic series—in addition to the invention cartoons that would come to define him—drawing an estimated fifty thousand comic strips.

Of cartooning, Rube said, *"Comic art is hard labor. . . . It is not so much the actual work of sketching in the figures in pencil and filling them out later in ink, but rather the daily drain upon your imagination."*

And still, somehow, his imagination wasn't drained. Rather, it was kicked into overdrive. Interspersed with his daily work as a cartoon artist, he also found time through the years to check off a few other accomplishments.

He made animated cartoons (seven of them!) and worked the vaudeville circuit (telling jokes and drawing cartoons) and published short stories and wrote TV scripts and film scripts (including *Soup to Nuts*, which introduced the Three Stooges to the world) and penned song lyrics and created cartoons for advertisers and founded the National Cartoonists Society and won the prestigious Pulitzer Prize (for a political cartoon) and published nonfiction articles and humorous essays. He wrote musicals! And finally, at the age of eighty, he decided to retire from his whirligig of a career . . . and then he became a sculptor.

"You have to have courage to be a creator," Rube said. *"It's all in the doing, and it shouldn't be talked about much."*

And "doing" was something Rube obviously did quite well—smashing expectations, crashing through obstacles, toppling creative boundaries, and rolling on to success. He was in constant motion . . . not unlike his invention contraptions: one thing to another thing and to still another. Smash, crash, topple, roll.

GLOSSARY

What Those Words Mean

actuating lever: a lever that is put into mechanical motion

chain reaction: a series of events, each triggered by the event that happened just before

contraption: a gadget or device, usually mechanical

effort: exertion; the use of physical energy to do something

energy: the capacity for doing work

force: a push or pull that will change an object's motion, if unopposed

friction: the resistance to motion of one object relative to another

fulcrum: the pivot point that a lever turns around

gadget: a small device with a practical use but that is usually a novelty

gravity: a fundamental physical force of attraction

kinetic: the energy an object has due to its motion

load: the force placed in or on an object

machine: a device for performing a task (mechanical, electric, or electronic)

mass: a property of an object based on how much matter (physical substance) it has

mechanical advantage: a measurement of the boost of force when a tool or machine is used

momentum: a property of a moving object based on the interaction of its mass with its velocity

Newton's laws of motion: three fundamental laws of physics that govern motion

patent: a legal document securing rights, often to an invention

physics: a branch of science that concerns the physical world

simple machines: the basic elements that apply force and that all machines are composed of

three-dimensional: having width, height, and depth

transfer of energy: when energy moves from one location to another (as in hitting a baseball with a bat), or when energy changes from one *form* to another (as in turning on a flashlight)

transfer of momentum: when momentum is transferred from one object to another object

two-dimensional: having width and height but not depth

velocity: how fast an object moves in a particular direction

work: a measure of energy transfer; the product of force and distance

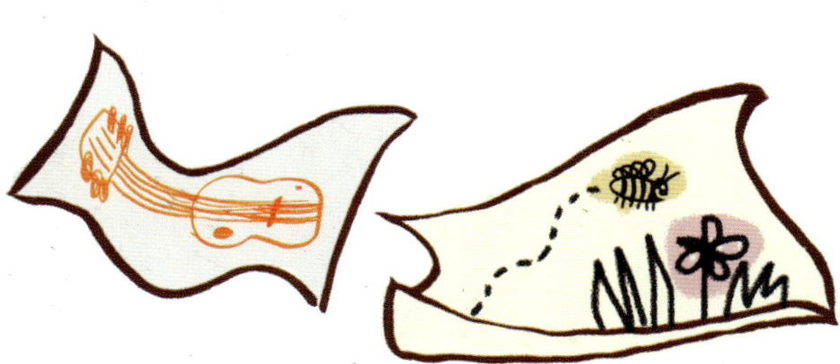

WATCH THIS!

Some Helpful Videos of Cool Contraptions

Search the internet using the prompts below to discover amazing videos of Rube Goldberg Machines in action:

fresh machine Target Rube video

Guinness World Record Rube Goldberg video

Honda cog

Joseph's Machines

Joseph's Machines page turner

light Christmas tree Rube

Melvin the Machine Rube

MythBusters Rube machine video

OK Go video Rube

Sprice AGT video

YouTube 75 chain reaction ideas

YOUR TURN!

Contests and Maker Spaces for YOU to Try

Make: Magazine
makezine.com

OK Go Sandbox
okgosandbox.org

SOURCES: QUOTATIONS, BOOKS, WEB PAGES, AND MORE

QUOTED AND PRIMARY SOURCES

Bahrainwala, Adam. Purdue University RGM contest winner; interview with the author.

Goldberg, Rube. "Comics, New Style and Old," *The Saturday Evening Post*, December 15, 1928.

Goldberg, Rube. "My Answer to the Question: How Did You Put It Over?" *American Magazine*, March 1922, pgs. 37–39, 64.

Goldberg, Rube. "Why I Am an Inventor (Do I Hear a Laugh?)," *Popular Science Monthly*, June 1923, pg. 27.

Kulash, Damian. OK Go lead singer; interview with the author.

Marzio, Peter C. *Rube Goldberg: His Life and Work*. Harper & Row, New York, 1973.

Merriam-Webster Dictionary. "Rube Goldberg," merriam-webster.com/dictionary/rubegoldberg. By permission from Merriam-Webster.com, © 2019 by Merriam-Webster, Inc.

Nathan, Emily. "Oral History Interview with Rube Goldberg," Archives of American Art, Smithsonian Institution, 1970.

Rube Goldberg papers, BANC MSS C-H 163, Box 3. Courtesy of The Bancroft Library, University of California, Berkeley.

Zukor, Arnold. Burglar alarm, US Patent 1,046,533, filed July 22, 1912, and issued December 10, 1912.

CONSULTED SOURCES

"Aged Sign Painter Inspires Goldberg," *Des Moines Register*, June 11, 1938.

Beschloss, Steven. "Object of Interest: Rube Goldberg Machines," *The New Yorker*, July 19, 2013.

Bloomfield, Louis A. *How Things Work: The Physics of Everyday Life*. 5th ed., Wiley, Hoboken, New Jersey, 2013.

CBS News. *Sunday Morning*, January 26, 2014 (segment on Rube Goldberg).

George, Jennifer, selected by. *The Art of Rube Goldberg: (A) Inventive (B) Cartoon (C) Genius*. Abrams ComicArts, New York, 2013.

Goldberg, Rube. "Inventions We Need in 1949," *Cosmopolitan*, January 1949.

Goldberg, Rube. "It's the Little Things That Matter," *Collier's*, November 3, 1928.

Goldberg, Rube, and Jane Dixon. "Hitting the Comics," *Top-Notch Magazine*, March 1 and 15, 1920.

Henle, Raymond. "Oral History Interview with Rube Goldberg," Rube Goldberg papers, The Bancroft Library, October 3, 1968.

Jamaica High School [New York]. *The Hilltopper*, March 26, 1941.

Keller, Charles, compiled by. *The Best of Rube Goldberg*. Prentice-Hall, Englewood Cliffs, New Jersey, 1979.

Kinnaird, Clark, edited by. *Rube Goldberg vs. the Machine Age: A Retrospective Exhibition of His Work with Memoirs and Annotations*. Hastings House, New York, 1968.

Snyder, Gerald S. "Hey, Rube!" *Stars and Stripes*, August 4, 1963, pg. 13.

Tumey, Paul. "Rube Goldberg Butts In," *The Comics Journal*, February 24, 2014.

Wolfe, Maynard Frank. *Rube Goldberg: Inventions*. Simon & Schuster, New York, 2000.

SELECT ONLINE SOURCES

Animation Is a Rube Goldberg Machine
huffpost.com/entry/animation-is-a-rube-goldb_b_5434284

Before OK Go: The History of Rube Goldberg Machines
brainpickings.org/2010/03/05/the-way-things-go

Brooklyn's Rube Goldberg
nytimes.com/video/nyregion/100000001266018/brooklyns-rube-goldberg.html

By Popular Demand: The OK Go Rube Goldberg Machine
hackaday.com/2010/03/20/by-popular-demand-the-ok-go-rube-goldberg-machine

History of the Rube Goldberg Machine Contest
purdue.edu/newsroom/rubegoldberg/history.html

How OK Go's Amazing Rube Goldberg Machine Was Built
wired.com/2010/03/ok-go-rube-goldberg

How to Engineer a Viral Music Video
ted.com/talks/adam_sadowsky_engineers_a_viral_music_video

The Incline, the Wedge, the Screw
hyperphysics.phy-astr.gsu.edu/hbase/Mechanics/incline.html

Introduction to Mechanical Advantage
khanacademy.org/science/physics/work-and-energy/mechanical-advantage/v/introduction-to-mechanical-advantage

Legacy of Rube Goldberg's Machines
rube-goldberg.com/wiki/legacy.html

Lever
newworldencyclopedia.org/entry/Lever

The Man behind the World's Biggest Rube Goldberg Machines Explains How You Control Chaos
jalopnik.com/the-man-behind-the-worlds-biggest-rube-goldberg-machine-5967389

Origin Stories: A History of Rube Goldberg Machines, and a List of the Best
junkee.com/origin-stories-rube-goldberg-machines/24645

The Physics of a Rube Goldberg Machine
colgatephys111.blogspot.com/2011/12/physics-of-rube-goldberg-machine.html

Rube Goldberg Contest—Rube Goldberg Machine
purdue.edu/newsroom/rubegoldberg

The Rube Goldberg Institute for Innovation and Creativity
rubegoldberg.org

Rube Goldberg on Inventions
youtube.com/watch?v=QQs4ZD3HjwQ

Rube Goldberg: The Man behind the Machines
https://gizmodo.com/rube-goldberg-the-man-behind-the-machines-5622673

Say, Are You Looking at a Computer? Rube Goldberg's Foolish Questions
screwballcomics.blogspot.com/2012/10/say-are-you-looking-at-computer-rube.html

Simple Machines
encyclopedia.com/social-sciences-and-law/economics-business-and-labor/businesses-and-occupations/simple-machines

Simple Machines
hyperphysics.phy-astr.gsu.edu/hbase/Mechanics/simmac.html

Simple Machines Explorations
youtube.com/playlist?list=PLHEILh2SIoI8l5XfLqRw-A_e_e1muv7JN

6 Kinds of Simple Machines
thoughtco.com/six-kinds-of-simple-machines-2699235

6 Simple Machines: Making Work Easier
livescience.com/49106-simple-machines.html

Taking Rube Goldberg Seriously
slate.com/technology/2014/04/rube-goldberg-heath-robinson-and-the-history-of-fictional-inventions.html

Talkin' Rube Goldberg with Author Jennifer George
huffingtonpost.com/tom-semioli/talkin-rube-goldberg-with_b_4537425

Who Says Machines Must Be Useful?
nytimes.com/2012/01/08/nyregion/brooklyns-joseph-herscher-and-his-rube-goldberg-machines.html

The World's Most Complicated Rube Goldberg Machine
popularmechanics.com/technology/a6668/the-worlds-most-complicated-rube-goldberg-machine

ZyynLabs Project Highlights
zyynlabs.com/projects

ACKNOWLEDGMENTS

Adam Bahrainwala, Purdue University, former student; Rutger Van Huber, physics and engineering consultant; Damian Kulash, OK Go; Bancroft Library staff; Smithsonian records researchers; marvelous editors Melissa Manlove and Jody Mosley; and the entire team at Chronicle Books.

CATHERINE THIMMESH is the award-winning author of many books for children, including *Team Moon*, winner of the Robert F. Sibert Medal, and *Camp Panda*, winner of a Robert F. Sibert Honor. *Madam President* was a New York Times Notable Children's Book. *Girls Think of Everything* won the IRA Children's Book Award and was a Children's Book of the Month Best Nonfiction Book, a Minnesota Book Award finalist, and a Smithsonian Notable Book for Children. Catherine lives in Eden Prairie, Minnesota.

SHANDA McCLOSKEY is the award-winning author and illustrator of STEM-friendly picture books like *Doll-E 1.0*, an NSTA Best STEM Book of the Year, and *T-Bone the Drone*, a Sunshine State Young Readers Award Jr. nominee. She is also cocreator of the *Author Visit Podcast* and Author Visit Central. Shanda lives in Ball Ground, Georgia. For more, visit www.shandamc.com.